DUST

BRADY PETERSON

ISBN: 978-0-9965405-2-0

Printed in the United States of America

Cover Design: RSCS
Cover Photo: Charley Peterson

Also by Brady Peterson:
Glued to the Earth
Between Stations

BIG TABLE Publishing

Big Table Publishing Company
Boston, MA
www.bigtablepublishing.com

Acknowledgments

Some of the poems in *Dust* appeared sometimes in a different form in the following publications:

The San Antonio Express: "The Light in an Again House" and "splinters"

Enigmatist: "Halo" and "Sunrise Pose"

Texas Poetry Calendar: "Gnarls" and "Leaving Sweetwater"

all roads will lead you home: "The Bell"

Boston Literary Magazine: "A Moral Imperative", "How Could We Not", and "Tuesday Morning"

The Good Men Project: "Boot Camp — 1967"

Blue Hole: "sunrise in Van Horn"

Windhover: "Redemption 1", "Redemption 2", and "Redemption 3"

The Journey of Military Experience: "Passing"

Table of Contents

For Melinda
who floats like a butterfly

& for Emily, Lou, Julie, and Charley
who help keep me glued to the earth

THE BELL

You and I, we talk this way—
as if the Earth were a street with coffee shops
and book stores, as if people lived deliberately,
about the funeral of an old friend and how the men,
dressed in dark suits, stood with their hands
crossed in front of them like wooden statues,

about how, despite loving me, you married Richard
when you were too young to know better,
then Robert who bought you a new Mercedes with money
he was going to make drilling for oil,
then finally Benjamin who hiked into the dense
forest of Costa Rica looking for the perfect coffee bean.

Benjamin, the best of them, you say with a grin,
looking directly into me, a talent you never lost—
as if the thread connecting the two of us was still
intact, and I believe it. How could I not believe
the implication in a smile, though
it was getting late.

DUST

April comes and goes—then May breeding
thunderstorms and twisters out of the sky—
storm chasers riding asphalt ribbons,
riding adrenaline—you call.

First responders digging through rubble, listening
for signs. You find yourself working triage,
separating the dying from those who might
be saved. You hold a woman's hand
and pray with her, time for a single prayer—

unaware the dust you are breathing—

Birds are singing this morning. So much depends—
He hopes for rain, a gully washer to the west
would be the preference, if he were only God—
though grateful to be spared that awful job.

He listens to the birds. He listen to the birds. He listens—

ANGEL

A boy stands outside a car window,
his hands and nose pressed against the glass.
The driver starts the engine–a December morning.
I don't want you to leave, he pleads, but there
is no choosing, only the sting.

His face fades into the fabric of stories
told when boys gather in a drainage
ditch between rains–about ghosts and spirits
lurking in the smoke of candles–about a man
who lives in the weeds behind the ice plant on the hill,
who snatches young boys unaware, eating
their fingers and toes.

You saw him once, you think–when you peddled
the steep hill on your bike, the first to the top,
the sun waning. A solitary figure rounds the corner
of the building, walking deliberately, a rush
when the imagined becomes flesh–

You turn your bike and flee,
peddling wildly down the hill,
losing control–

A mango tree grows into a giant–they live
hundreds of years. You are standing in a road
where a boy pressed his nose against a car window
and cried.

THE LIGHT IN AN AGING HOUSE

Anything below the knees or above the head
goes unnoticed for the most part, though we make
the bed. The floors are crusty, and cobwebs
decorate the corners of the ceiling. We find peace
with this arrangement, she and I.

There's the woman in the tub with her russet
sponge, but only I seem to see her, kneeling
with her back to me. The toes on her left foot,
the fingers on her left hand. I brush my teeth
while she bathes.

The vinyl flooring curls next to the tub,
pried loose once by an invading tree root seeking
moisture and threading its web from the commode
like some organic tapestry. My plumber cut
the root but gave no guarantee as to its return.

Imprints remain on the concrete slab. Degas
invites me to coffee. It's too early for dancers.

A MORAL IMPERATIVE

You wonder about the notion of choosing–
do we ever. Dumping jeans and t-shirts
in a washing machine on a Saturday morning
already fading into noon, already losing
the feel of Saturday. Do we watch football

or take a walk down the road, playing chicken
with the cars, the shoulder barely wide enough,
tilting down–there was a time, we tell
ourselves, when it was quiet here, when one
could hear the breeze–the game still playing

when we return. We pick a side,
eeny, meeny, miny, moe–
You remember an October evening, sitting
in the stands and watching a last minute
touchdown secure defeat or victory depending,

later eating a hamburger and fries in a roadside
café, the jukebox playing, your uncle leaning
in and telling you he was a Hank Williams man–
a former Baptist preacher selling booze
in your father's liquor store,

and who one Friday during Christmas season,
dressed up as a red headed Mrs. Claus and stood
on the giant stuffed rabbit sitting in front
of the store parking lot, a landmark of sorts,
waving at the cars going by.

ISCARIOT

There is no coming back, you understand–
redemption being just a word–once you cross
the line. It's drawn somewhere–in the sand, etched
in stone, somewhere–a line munching
on a toenail or two.

Moan and complain if you want–about the game
being rigged, about dreary winters, snow turning
to slush–about how your mother never really
loved you–your father bloated and jaundiced,
the sweet hint of whiskey on his breath,

a stubble of whiskers scratching your lips
when you lean down to kiss him.

You look for a bakery in the morning before dawn,
the yeasty smell of bread baking–a roll and a cup
of coffee being an absolution of some kind.
You confess sins to the woman behind the counter,
standing in for a priest, and she smiles and hands
you a white paper bag.

WHAT WE HAVE

This is what we have—
cereal and milk with a banana
sliced in—black coffee.

It's always coffee with you,
a student once told him
after reading his poems.

A sacrament—berries grown
in the mountains of a remote farm,
picked by hand when ripe,

one at a time. Dried in the sun,
then carried in burlap bags
down the slopes.

Shipped to New Orleans or Houston—
Roasted only a week before grinding,
ground only minutes

before brewing—only the first sip
really tasting fresh.
Inadequate, yet necessary.

WALKING EARLY TO WORK

A whimsical but clear synaptic firing
weighs on the heart like a slab of bacon
cooked to grease and sopped with a biscuit
on a late December morning. He walks
the sidewalk to the plant, before the sun–

I snuggle with my new baseball
glove, fitting my right hand, the smell
of leather, the scent of a pipe
tobacco lingering in the house–
The choice of scrambled eggs

or fried, one or two, coffee with milk
and sugar–somehow thinking the world
would never turn, that all was right
and good and solid, the stinging cold
of linoleum on bare feet.

IT RAINS

It rains, it doesn't rain, we grumble either way,
the nature of the toad. I dreamed you wanted
to kiss me last night, only we couldn't find a place,
a recurring theme—my kingdom for a room
in a not so cheap motel, he cries.

People scurry in and out, some guy fishing
a stream using a giant umbrella as a net,
your whispering in my ear something about
the last chapter in a book I haven't read.
Remember, you tell me, only—

I wake to the sanity of an empty bed,
check my watch after fixing my trifocals
to my nose. Just a few minutes more,
he pleads as if he were begging for scraps
to be dropped from a table.

THE FALL

Rain splatters against the table tops
on the deck at Mozart's. We are trapped inside,
drinking coffee, yours sprinkled with cinnamon,
drowned in half and half.

You are reading about the Alamo.
I am reading the exodus of Paris when it is already
too late. Madame Pericand tells Jacqueline
with a discreet gesture to share the lollipops in her bag

and feels a sense of satisfaction, being so charitable.
You put your head down on the open book.
Crockett arrives in time to die. Bowie dies.
Travis, hot head to the end, traces a line in the dirt

with a sword–or a stick. You look up
then put your head down again.
Houston, knowing his Napoleon, retreats–
biding his time.

My cousin Buddy tells you–as tragic
as the Alamo was–the slaughter of all those
Texicans–everyone alive that March day,
all the people in England and China too–

WHEN ALL ELSE FAILS

The wounds, like cracks on an eggshell—
my mother once described it that way, what love
does to the heart, never healed for her, never scarred
over stronger than before.

Little by little her heart was irreparably broken.
Humpty fell—and all the king's horses,
all the king's men—

She left notes for me to find,
tucked away in the back of a drawer,
in a book partially read,
in a side pocket of a purse.

Why couldn't we have been happy,
she mumbled, trying to make sense of a life
as we sat side by side in the uncomfortable
chairs of a hospital waiting room.

I leaned closer and whispered,
do you remember the time you peed
your pants when you almost ran
over that armadillo.

She snorted a grin
while staring at the floor.

MoMA

The narrative escapes us. There is no point
to the man standing alone on a platform
in a station waiting for the train, his hands
in his pockets, the bitter cold stinging
his cheeks. He is not coming home,
nor going to work, nor meeting his wife.
He is only standing alone on a platform,
waiting. Nothing happens. No one comes
up to him to ask the time or to discuss
the imperatives of existence. He listens
to the wind, his hands in his pockets.

A HOLDING PATTERN

The birds find a way to get inside
the netting and peck tiny holes in his ripening
tomatoes. He could pick them sooner
and let them ripen on the counter,
but that would miss the whole point
of working dirt into food.

Tomato, onion, dill–He plays the words
on his tongue, crushing a basil leaf, rubbing
it between finger and thumb, presses it to his nose
and inhales the tones. Here one can almost feel–
here on the edge of falling.

He sleeps under a fan and sweats the night
into his sheets, the window cracked enough
to let in the sound of a car passing,
his wife breathing next to him, too hot
for touching, living by choice.

He showers cold in the morning and climbs
into his shorts without toweling. Brews coffee
with beans grown and picked in the mountains
in Nicaragua. The flat screen news,
part of the ritual. There, a man in a tailored suit
is preaching sin to a nation turned against God.

OM

It rained rivers yesterday, a temporary reprieve,
and you let yourself believe it will hold back the desert
a little longer. Though it's too late to save the big oaks.

The birds are busy this morning, hopping the limbs
in the remaining trees, chirping. So much depends,
you mutter under your breath…

The red wheelbarrow is tucked under the eave
of the back porch, the potted tomato sprouts
left on the open patio are beaten down a little,

but happy. It's too muddy to weed the garden,
too muddy to do anything but breathe and listen.
You sip your coffee and read a while.

DRIP

Geese are flying south—
in a line this morning, angled
slightly, taking turns,
the first I've seen this year.

Dew drips from the eaves
of my metal roof, the sun
making another appearance
as if to guarantee today

and thus tomorrow, though
my daughter reminds me
not to eat fish caught in the Pacific
for a few years or more.

I pour a fresh cup and count
the ways—I listen to cars
passing by my window, someone
driving to work, or to a doctor's

office, to the store, school—
or maybe to meet a lover in a park
below the dam. I passed a couple
meeting there once and envied

them, my morning run intersecting
bits of conversation.

HAMLET ORDERS BREAKFAST

I just don't get old English,
she says as if to underscore
her problem with Bill and more
to the point her inability to pay
the rent this month–

He sighs and tries to explain
the difference between Tyndale
and Beowulf, but times are hard,
and she was stiffed by a sweet talking
old woman yesterday at work

who claimed to have left her checkbook
in the car, then never came back.
They do that more than you would think,
she says, and I always seem to fall
for it when they smile and talk sweet.

ASHES

The archaeology of digging into a pile
of burnt cans and bottles in the gully behind
the back garden plot of turnips and butter beans,
finding a blue bottle with squared edges in the heap–
unbroken–thinking it once contained some magic potion.

A gypsy camp just down the road, a place
forbidden though we were never told–yet we knew.
Women in red bandanas, dogs yelping in the morning air,
smoke rising from tin colored trailers.   December–
We wear coats ordered from a catalogue.

A '52 Buick, two toned green,
parked on the dirt ruts in the brown grass
beside the old house. We place the blue bottle
on a cross plank of the clothes line post
and use it as a target for our bb guns.

FREELANCE RECORDINGS

Still, he could hear it,
just below the hum of tires,
some indecipherable code,

a random tapping
picked up on an old frequency,
hanging like the floater

in his eye. A presence,
but not something
he could easily explain.

Much of it ends up this way,
the reshaping of a story
until no one listens.

There were no arrests in the middle
of the night, nor in the middle
of the day. No one was led

away. There was no God,
only the high priests
standing in their robes.

He watches another scene
fold into itself
like burning paper.

A small girl loses touch
with a mother's hand
and wanders into the crowd.

He listens for her to cry out.

ARIA

I dreamed last night we spoke, you and I,
sharing a moment, though a moment is all.
My morning throat crusty, eyes a little red,
five o'clock in a hotel with the AC humming.
I brew a packet of god awful coffee,

worse than I remember freeze dried
instant being. An aging swollen face in a bathroom
mirror, the one you said was cute
in my dream, though I was old there too.
Still you said I was cute and smiled.

The dream is lost in the stacks of a tower
library before they moved the books to the new
one, lost between two dusty tomes, in the AC hum,
in the taste of really bad coffee. I try to retrieve
it from the shelves, but I can't remember–

LEAVING SWEETWATER

Wind turbines crowd the horizon
like a white stubble of whiskers
on an old face. He is driving northwest,
past pterodactyl heads without wings,
bobbing for apples.

He passes a sign: *Don't make me come
down there–God.* White lettering
on black. He reaches in the sack
on the passenger seat and retrieves
a spice drop. Sugar keeps him awake.

He is hours and miles from the mountains.
A man on the radio talks about living
the intentional life in Christ. We decided
our one focus would be on our finances,
a woman explains, as if money saved

were the key–he switches stations,
picks up a signal embedded in the asphalt road,
the gravel voice of the Wolfman beckoning
from Acuña.

THE MISSION

She inherited her mother's heart,
the muscle not the song.
Her mother died when
she was still young, she tells you
one evening when you are standing
outside the library, leaning against car
doors and absorbing the moon.

I want to see my grandchildren married,
she says, so she does what she can
to keep breathing, to keep the pump
working. Diet and exercise,
the mantra—but seeking something more
as she trudges up a mountain side
in Nicaragua, chasing the ghost of Sandino,
to see in the faces of the people who live
closer to the earth… to hear in their laughter
the sound of rain splattering against
a canopy of leaves.

MOLOCH

Ginsberg is a waste of time,
the kid behind me in line for barbecue
says in a smug tone, as if he knew
something more. Unless you want
to read about lurid romps
in cheap hotels, he adds slightly bored.

When the old guard from the 60s and 70s
who still worship this asshole die off,
we will be rid of him–thank God.
Lunch at a writers festival. I order
brisket, slaw, potato salad.

Vonnegut, who despised City Lights
and the beat writers, claimed
everyone knew the best minds majored
in engineering not English.

Lost in the moment, Vonnegut emerges
from a slaughter house locker
to find Dresden burnt to a crisp.

HALO

A bird outside my window chirping–
I think it's a glitch in my computer, an annoyance
until I realize–fragile notes, a morning
sun rising on a Wednesday.

I was thinking it Tuesday–losing
a day somewhere. It's easy in February
to lose track–days or weeks–
The rye grass green and unmowed–

Here cold is a long sleeve shirt
on most days. I walk barefoot to retrieve
the morning paper I seldom bother
to unroll. Obituaries go unread–

the passing of someone I might
have known before–before the eclipse
before the storm–before, when we would meet
at the Blue Moon Cafe on a Saturday morning

after a Friday night game and drink coffee with cream
and sugar–not the way I drink it now–
and listen to the talk of some defensive tackle
who played for the school in the late fifties

and who died in a crash at a railway crossing–
playing chicken with God, a friend of your
father says, and everyone nods.
You smile at me.

A SNAPSHOT

A photograph snapped at twenty-six
in a mountain park north of Logan,
his blond hair glistening, wearing
a p-coat, knowing this was his best day.

His daughter, only two, tags along
and points to a man sporting a beard–
Look, a monkey, she squeals. A monkey.
The man doesn't seem amused.

The image slightly out of focus,
an October day–John invites
him to stay, but the urge is pulling
him somewhere else.

HE WAKES UP IN PHOENIX

In dreams, I ride my bicycle
from my home in Texas
to my wife's home in Southern California
and back a dozen times or more,
peddling under Sugarloaf in El Paso,
stopping for lunch at *Si Senor's*
in Deming, tasting the difference
in New Mexican cuisine.

I am eleven when our troop explores
an abandoned tin mine–camping
in a desert mountain chain. A half mile in,
we turn off our flashlights and listen
to the walls.

Crazy Bill tells me, sipping beer
under a single bright bulb dangling above
a kitchen table, that in the bush–
in Nam, when the night was overcast,
he couldn't see his fingers no matter
how close he held them to his face.
I shot a dog one night, he says, thinking
it was the enemy.

LITERARY CRITICISM DURING AND AFTER THE WAR

a rumor caught between days
restricted to reacting to his father's
thinking   a closed maze

assimilated into the cozy
warmth of believing we have
emerged from the belly of the dragon
asleep for now   or long dead

reciting jingles   jingles all the way
oh, what fun   good to the very
very last drip   drip
hand to the heart   inserting under God

to make it holy   he runs from shadows
spreading across the map   like ink
spilled   the fabric fraying at the edges
his blurting out suddenly   without warning

how deeply he loved   how he walked
the streets alone at night muttering your name
to the angels   how he tried to escape
through the mountains into Spain

but was held for questioning   I know absolutely
nothing, he cries   when the dragon
walks into the room

ASYLUM

A stack of books tumbles from the leaf
on my desk, the slightest nudge from my elbow
the culprit, and a clump of pages from Anne's
poems slips from the cover, the binding glue failing
months ago, years ago—the pages like bed sheets

washed and flapping on the line where
she watches them, then buries her head in them—
though really lying on the floor like
children shot in an elementary school,
very still, very quiet.

I look for the poem about Anne in Paris.
She is walking the streets imagining yesterday
1890, imagining 1940 never happened,
writing to her Nana who wrote letters
from Paris when she was young, yesterday—

before she grew old and constipated.
Anne sits in her room with her 58 lbs. of books.
A nudge from my elbow and jackboots
thump through the Paris streets.

A CONCERTO

He never played the clarinet well enough
to lose himself in the music–the notes on the page
becoming sounds in his head–struggling to hold
the embrasure, counting measures, fingering the keys–
more complicated than a golf swing–but well enough
to know–to feel the swell of intent.

Outside, chainsaws are gnawing the dead limbs
on his oak. Inside, he sits at his desk listening to Mozart–
trying to reconcile the two. The dog cowers between
his feet–he wants to explain to the dog who only wants
to be petted.

LANDFILL

We back the pickup to the edge of the pit,
the bed stuffed with a witches brew–a worn mattress,
cans of old paint, a dog piss stained carpet–
assorted treasures left behind by a tenant
slipping out on Wednesday and promising to someday
pay the back rent–you've been too good to us,
she says with round earnest eyes–
a commode too black for muriatic acid to clean.

Later in the day we sit on the porch and drink
cold Shiner and talk about times before seatbelts,
when gas was thirty cents a gallon, about the carpenter
who had slipped out on our tenant a few months earlier,
leaving her with back rent and a black commode.

CANARY

a clipping tacked to a cork board
in the kitchen–yellowed–
about a mother of four running down
her husband in a neighbor's front yard,
not her mother who never bothered,

when losing herself in the pages
of a book no longer kept her from falling
through the gaps in the narrative,
when on a clear day–chasing him over
the curb in her minivan with six payments

still due, through the periwinkles–
he trips on a sprinkler head,
a thud in a less traveled storyline–
the neighbors saying they always
suspected something was amiss

WRITING ITS OWN HISTORY

They cut off his hands after killing him,
shooting him nine times in the legs
and arms, then chest, then throat,
begging the question—brutal pipe
smoking motorcycle dreaming bastard—

He asked for tobacco from a common
soldier who offered him a pouch,
and he thanked the soldier—the dark
sin of siding with miners and peasants—
and the band played on filling the space

while we sat at a bar in a Monterey
hotel wondering if the woman,
wearing a pretty face, talking quietly
to the bartender, would look our way
and smile.

IF EVER

standing at a podium, wearing suspenders
over a white shirted bulging belly,
a confessed smoker, speaking in earth tones,
he tells us, reminds us really, that being
a good and decent person won't keep the hounds at bay—

not anymore—if ever. a mother fox cuts
across the trail, trying to steer the dogs away
from her young. she listens for the howling,
signifying her pups are safe, but the dogs
don't turn—

the buzz of a pilotless drone overhead
in the dark—the citizens of Melos
appealing to the Athenian sense of justice
and mercy—the infrared imprint of a small human
on a screen cooling—

REQUIEM

He listens to a requiem in d minor,
each note working to slow the racing in his head,
a mass for the dead   of winter.
It snows here, she tells him,
and he didn't bring his overcoat   or gloves.

Lovely, he sighs, always prepared
for the calamity
looming like a ghoul painted
above the entrance of a carnival ride,
the girl clutching his arm.

Slipping off the track,   his mind skims
the surface of the water,   a small fish
even here.   Just a minnow, he mutters.
A leaf falls to the street during a break
in the performance.

SAND CREEK

Purity, like innocence,
is an obscenity we fail
to fully comprehend.
Instead we descend
like angels in the fog
of morning, like angels
wearing heavy coats,
before the rooster crows,
bearing down on those
still sleeping, unaware
that the moment has slipped
from their grasp.

FEEDING THE CHISHOLM

Everything is history—ruts worn into limestone
by chuck wagon wheels on a slope nearby,
the smell of cattle settling into dirt,
a sweat stained cotton shirt, a thunder cloud
rising in an otherwise clear sky.

The trek to Abilene bringing ten fold
the value of a steer—ticks and mesquite
part of the baggage. Faces chiseled by gritty
wind and by the long war behind them now—
the rumbling of distant thunder.

PINNED

Miranda yearns for sunlight—
locked away in Frederick's cellar.
He calls himself Ferdinand,
obsessed with the notion—belief
if she only knew him.

Caliban, she scribbles in her journals
as she grows paler—Caliban the monster,
Caliban the ordinary man who captures
specimens for his collection, Caliban
without Prospero to check him.

He proposes to her at a Ranger game,
in front of the world, Jim Knox holding
the microphone, all of it on the screen—
how could she say no.
If she only knew him, he thinks.

RETHINKING

While the world may be redeemed–
that is, if we accept–
      confess–   receive–

he wonders still, if it could
      just be reset–

Not flooded like before
when, if you subscribed,
the dinosaurs vanished–

too many drowned.

Nor burnt in purging fires–
he sighs for Tyndale–
for Servetus–predestined for hell.

A blinding light–
      a young girl climbs onto
a crowded bus.

A single breath. A simple turning off,
then on again.

SIGNS

He listens to the raspy caws
of three crows as he walks
the empty streets of a still
unfamiliar town. Large dark
birds silhouetting an evening sky,
the naked fingers of trees,
messengers of Odin
or the souls of murdered men,
either way, a hollow omen
for nothing good.

Hands in his pocket, counting
to twenty on beads imagined,
muttering incantations
against the chill. A crow lands
on a tree branch and watches
him.

HAWK

a white flash of an under wing as it tilts
in the air, more muscular than a turkey vulture,
more solitary–

they walk the dam overlooking
the blue lake water, hiding the old asphalt road
and the once plowed fields where she had slipped quietly
out of her nylon underwear on a particular chilly night
some fifty years past–he had almost drowned
in the river one summer afternoon when a cold beer
and a strong current–

but now they are admiring a hawk soaring,
and they are walking the dam, appeasing
a modestly high blood pressure and an aging
spread, neither wanting any of it back.

GNARLS

The mesquite taproot
burrows itself a hundred

feet or more
into the ground

and sucks the land
so dry that one time

streams are reduced
to stone. A divining

rod provides little
in the way of guidance,

no dips, no sudden jerks
to the left or right.

And under a mid-
afternoon sun,

he strikes a rock
once with a crooked

stick, then again
for good measure,

as if the gesture
could alter the equations

so carefully written
into the parched earth.

FIRST SMILE

His grandmother hangs a dozen white chickens
on a clothes line, then beheads them with a knife.
They flap upside down, creatures in a nursery
rhyme, squawking without sound–He watches
from a distance.

The school perched up the hill with swings in front,
windows like eyes–Plays tackle football without pads
one winter when he's nine–back from the island,
the school being a way station–the taste of grass
and blood on his lips.

When he's six, by the swings, he tells the world
and the two girls playing with him, Pat is his girlfriend,
and she smiles. A simple declaration, the grin an affirmation.
When he's twelve, he watches her play basketball in the old
gym, the ground having shifted.

YESTERDAY

Two bald eagles circle overhead
as we take our morning walk,
the first I've seen in the wild–

We walk looking up until we are dizzy
and then walk looking up even more–
Majestic is the word you use,

and though it's inadequate, I can't conjure
a better one. It's a sign for peace and luck,
a cousin writes from Alaska–

at least here it is, she tells us. Something
more, another affirms. We have this need,
it seems, for signs and assurances,

as if an eagle is not an eagle or a butterfly
is not a butterfly, but a connection
to a realm beyond this one.

The sky is so blue, not even a vapor trail
this morning–

WINTER

I am lost.
Frost hazes the window,
icicles hang from the eaves,

though there is no pot stirring,
no crackling fire in Ada's
front room when I was ten

where one could freeze and blister
simultaneously. Here cold is quiet,
a dreamless sleep.

An owl lands on a tree branch—listen.
An owl lands on a tree branch,
then flies from the branch to our feet

on a Thursday evening after class
while we stand in a parking lot.
Oh my God, you say.

I sit alone in a room, trying to remember
when winters were cold. I sit alone
in a room, writing to you, trying to remember

the song playing the afternoon we walked
to where your mother was to pick you up.
You turn—listen, you say.

You climb into the car and look back,
wearing a blue and white scarf,
playing a perfect goodbye,

my standing at the curb.

NECESSITY

They watch two coyotes run across
the construction site of another subdivided dream.
He hears them bark at night when his window
is cracked–here, not far from the Chisholm,
where cattle chewed grass while heading for Kansas.

It is cold this morning. The heater clicks on.
The house creaks as if haunted. It always has, his sister
tells him one afternoon years ago. They discuss
exorcism using rock'n roll with the volume up.
The dead hate The Stones.

The coyotes stop and gaze their way.
He tries to grab an Annie Dillard weasel moment,
an exchange of souls, the point of view flipping–
imagines himself scampering over the graded roadbeds
toward the dam.

TUESDAY

Weeping greets me this morning
before coffee, before getting up to piss,
before the birds start haggling over a piece
of tree branch or whatever they find
so essential.

A dream lingers but is losing
its shape–I am fitted
for a suit jacket, having shown up inappropriately
dressed. A man in a buttoned vest measures my sleeve.
I am standing in the middle of an empty room.

I know this man–It is Tuesday,
garbage day. I roll out of bed still wearing
clothes from the night before, slip
into my sandals, bag the kitchen trash–
carry it to the bin which I roll to the curb.

My neighbor's garbage is already there.
His pit bull watches me from its pen
but doesn't bark. I pick up the paper–
head back into the house. We never speak,
my neighbor and I.

Inside, my wife has already made the bed
and is in the shower.

A CHANCE MEETING

They walk the drag on a morning in June—
browse through the wares of street vendors,
a wooden propeller on a stick—
She spins it between her palms, and it flies
ten feet or more into the air.

She catches the image of two people in a storefront
window and forgets for a moment—
I thought they made a nice couple, she says
as they sit outside Whole Foods some years later,
counting grackles perched on power lines.

A reflection without
the complications of narrative—
If only she had met him in Mexico.
I remember your coming to class late
every day, she says, wearing your white hat

and carrying a backpack over your shoulder—
before backpacks were commonplace.
She walks him to his bike.

A BIRTHDAY

Grilled steaks and margaritas
made with limes, a reposado,
Cointreau, and ice–shaken with vigor,
meat cooked medium rare–

His own at three–his father pulls a red fire truck
from the trunk of their Packard–
the neighbor kids take turns riding and pushing.

His father leaves for Japan,
a side of the closet empty the next morning.

He traces time spent in a converted
nineteenth century mercantile store,
thick adobe walls, wooden planked floors–
sipping margaritas and getting thoroughly drunk

on just two. I'm drunk, let's make another,
she grinned. No, he said and grinned back.
They talked about living on the beach–
walking thigh deep in the surf.

IN DREAMS

Henry is cross with god, or is it John–
the generation wrecked, but how could it not–
what with the war raining phosphorus,
cooking bones to ash–Delmore
stands in a theatre, cries out

it's not too late. He is ushered up the aisle
and out the door. It's not too late, don't
you see, he cries–the smell of napalm
on a Cambridge morning, don't you see–
How do the prosperous live with themselves,

he asks. He reaches for the key to a cheap
hotel room–abandoned by his friends,
by the gods–disheveled and thin,
he falls to the carpeted floor outside his room,
the key inserted but unturned.

TUESDAY MORNING

He passes my window in the morning, tall–angular
with ebony skin, a white beard, walking his dog.
Sometimes I meet him on the road. He raises his hand
acknowledging my presence, heels the dog
with a soft command. I nod.

He strides like an old gunny, knowing where and when,
though he is only walking the dog down the road,
around the park next to the dam. I watch him
from my window and wonder if we might have been friends
in a life forgotten, drinking coffee at a cafe on a Saturday
morning, talking about the weather or a football game,
or the moon.

Something that pulls me to admire him–maybe even love him,
maybe the gait of his step, the way the dog walks by his side
with the leash dragging the ground behind, the two of them
being enough.

THIS IS WHAT WE DO

This is what we do, she says,
driving him to the funeral home
where they are to pick up the urn—
ashes of a man who once climbed
a mountain in Chili at seventy-five.

A thirtyish woman wearing a black skirt, white blouse,
and smile hands them a brushed gold metal box
and folded flag. A release to be signed.
We attend the dead and the dying, she means—
and he mutters something about riding his bicycle

in the morning air, about walking the beach
barefoot, trousers rolled—about drinking a beer
in the evening at a bar in the plaza, talking
to the bartender, a tri-cut beef salad roll—topping
off the conversation with a shot of tequila

and a dab of jalapeno lime liqueur. This one's on me,
the bartender says as he wipes the counter.
Three days earlier he lifts the man from his bed—frail,
unable to move one arm—frail yet clinging—
light yet heavy as lead.

WE ONCE PLAYED

We once played baseball unsupervised,
climbed trees, squatted in culverts
between rains–played war,
using sticks as guns, jumped out of swings.

A college friend of my oldest daughter fell
from a cliff one afternoon–free climbing.
A college friend of mine was killed in Nam
when his jeep rolled over a bomb.

Another slammed head on into a truck
while driving home to see if his high school
girl friend was pregnant. We had stayed
up all night talking. He fell asleep.

The week before, we played catch in a parking
lot and talked about trying out as walk-ons
in the spring. Johnny and I boxed his clothes
and books, told his father why he was driving home

that morning. Johnny was in the jeep–in Nam.
My third daughter found his name on the wall
during Christmas break this year. The girlfriend
had twins, we were told.

I fix a split pea soup with onions and ham shanks–
brown rice. My wife tells me she had a better day
at school by just reminding herself her boys
would rather be playing baseball unsupervised.

BOOT CAMP–1967

He climbs the ramp, turns before entering
the plane and sees one of his new buddies kissing
his girlfriend goodbye. She is wearing the first
miniskirt he had seen, her long legs telling
him with certainty his life had taken a wrong turn–

Oh shit, he finds himself muttering
the entire flight to Chicago. Shit, as they ride
the bus from O'Hare after spending the night
in the terminal–A girl wearing a brown
coat, boots, and a red and white scarf climbs

on the bus and sits in the seat across the aisle.
He doesn't know if she's pretty or not, it's enough
she is sitting across the aisle. He steals a glance,
and she smiles at him–the beginning and end
of an affair he will carry in his coat pocket

as if it were a letter to be read at night
in the head–the only light burning. At night
when everyone was asleep, he sits cross legged
on the hard deck in his skivvies–
It is snowing outside. Morning comes at four am.

ON COLLEGE STREET

A boy, three or four, picks up
a worm, brought to the surface by a recent
rain and holds it between his fingers and thumb.

The mailman reads a postcard
sent from a soldier to his wife who rents
an apartment in the back part of a house

owned by a blind man. In an open field
men play baseball after work—the war
on the peninsula being only a distant rumor.

An old man drives his horse drawn wagon
up the street—the children taunt him with a common
chant—his head down, eyes glued to the road,

shoulders slumped, the whiskers white on his chin,
feinting deaf and dumb. DiMaggio plays
for the Yankees in a world made safe—

TAKING INFIELD

The sound of rain on a metal roof
like childhood in a good dream
where he still—with chocolate and coffee—
the splatters of rain—I imagine you alive,
emerging from your house

as we wait for the bus to take us to school—
your red hair—It's raining harder now
a distant flash and then a grumbling
from the old gods—We once kneeled
to them, sang to them, burned offerings—

The last time I saw you, I was playing baseball,
he says. If you saw me, you hid it well—
sitting in the back seat of a car parked on the road
beside the park. We are taking infield—
A child wakes in an adjoining room. Whimpers—

then faint voices behind a door—You were ten,
and Jack, who taught us more than allowed,
was already packing to move, as would we in a week—
to Oklahoma. You emerge from your house
in January—the mountains in the distance

MORE THAN ONCE

Of course I've loved more than once,
he confesses offhandedly, unconcerned
with trifling betrayals–the old betraying
the new, or the other way around–he grins
and sips his coffee black, it being morning

and too early for agave, his being too old
to weigh ancient grudges with any seriousness.
Nothing is all that special–and everything,
he wants to tell the woman sitting across the room
who briefly considers his gaze and smiles,

but then turns back to the book she has been
reading–or pretending to read–a prop perhaps…
and his companion, an old friend who knew him
before one of them had died, grins from a story
told in a letter. Shot in the head by an enraged brother

one night when booze and entropy had intersected,
his grabbing a pistol from his brother's hand the first
go around, being once a prized college wrestler–
The brother leaves. He sits slumped at a kitchen table,
thinking it is over.

SUNRISE IN VAN HORN

wondering if we turned right toward Marfa,
recent rains painting the stretched out land
with a green tint, a truck stop on the Interstate,
a cup of stale coffee and a nuked gooey breakfast
burrito–filling the tank with gas

and hesitating at the junction, however briefly–
what if we turned right toward Marfa
for just the sound of it–

SUBLIMATION

he settles into a morning ritual   do you believe
anymore   no, he says   palm to palm,
pressed lightly against his nose   yet he poses
as if   in his hands   a cardinal lands
on a branch outside his window   January comes cold

rain drips from the eaves   like tears
Thomas who died a few days ago   another down
in a game of musical chairs   a man flogged
outside the mosque   fifty lashes
but he does not cry out

holding in a still room   the space between
worlds   do you believe anymore   no, he says
yet he clings to the thought of seeing in another,
no matter the circumstance,   an echo of the urge,
the yearning

SPLINTERS

a screen door opens,
and you find a certain peace in commonplace
luxuries–a wooden plank floor,
dust on a window sill–a red plum
picked from a bin after a light squeeze–

your hands rough from pulling lumber,
stacking and binding it for Walt who handles
a forklift like a soft shoe dancer–the yeasty
smell of bread rising in the ovens at a neighboring
bakery–Walt, who must be dead by now

or almost a hundred years old, slips the fat
metal forks under the stack of long boards–
a balancing act–between orders you pick
dewberries growing on the edges of the yard
and put them in an empty coffee can

SKIMMERS

on a boat made of grass
or carved from tree trunks,
sails out past line of sight,
past the edge of the world–
this urge,

the madness of genetic code,
he reads in Kolbert when his coffee
has cooled–a scone on his plate
in a market on north Lamar–he waits
for Bob to show after a month

in India–we fly there now in sardine
cans–they talk for twenty years
over a second and third cup, friends
for forty, or longer if you count
in middle English–

EIGHTH GRADE

We collect quarters for Dr. Tom Dooley,
believing as we do in the mosaic of Coca Cola
and rag top Chevrolets–a primary in West Virginia
proving that even a Catholic could–

Trouble is brewing at a Woolworth, but nothing
that couldn't wait, my mother says, adding Rome
wasn't built–We listen to Sam Cooke
and play basketball at the rec center on base,

the squeaking of rubber soles on hardwood
floors, learning to pick and roll, driving left
and passing the ball to David breaking open–
David who later kisses my date at the banquet.

BEING

A mockingbird lands on the wire cage
of a tomato plant, ruffles its feathers,
and flies off. The droppings on the leaves
suggest a ritual for the bird.

He watches as if dreaming,
detached from the man drinking
coffee. Listens as if dreaming.
This morning he woke to thunder

rumbling outside his cracked window,
the thunder making love to the earth. He sits
on his back porch and watches a mockingbird
land on the wire cage of a tomato plant.

AN EVENING IN OCTOBER

You might see in his eyes,
if you look, the remnants of desire,
but don't be fooled as he hits
you for a cheeseburger
and fries with ketchup.

It's the ketchup he loves.
You eat and listen to the blues
being played in a backroom.
Do you dance, he asks.
No, you tell him.

The golden frog is dying in Panama,
he says. Imagine a world without them.
You bite into your cheeseburger
and nod as if you were listening.
I can dance, you finally say somewhere

in the evening.

A SUMMER JOB

working for a sixty a week,
dusty and worn at the edge,
carrying brick and wheeling mud
up a 2 x12 ramp–a tight rope dance
to an R&B song while the ΣAE guy
keeps time on a clipboard–

Mitchell, the crew supervisor, appears
at the liquor store at night and hangs
for an hour or two, talking to his mother,
buys a pint and leaves–

to the crew, he is rabbit–at college
they call him gator, not a compliment,
but it works as they slurp black coffee
after supper and talk about how they
sure as hell didn't want to work construction
all their life–sure as hell–

after work, full of grit, he sees her dancing
with another guy–isn't it always that way,
and he can't help but cut in–

A SACRAMENT

He has a new smoker, bought for hamburgers
after the baptism of his two newest granddaughters—
after the sermon on learning to forgive—
you never—on not holding grudges—
after the music, after the prayers—

Do you believe in prayer, he says to her—I did
for a long time—We have grown old together,
you and I—despite our best efforts.
His son-in-law rolls the hamburger patties
in a mixture of coarse salt and spices, coating the edges—

She looks back—*an unforgivable sin*—turns
to keep from falling. They cook the meat
off center, away from the coals. He sips his beer,
his feet planted firmly, feels the earth
floating—

A CONFESSION

The moon smiles
for no particular reason,
perched above the tree line,

and I am pissing on the grass
behind my house which is more
satisfying, I think, than stealing pears.

In Carlsbad once, I listened
to a physician tell me about a real
estate agent showing him a property

outside of Houston, pointing to the advantage
of country life. Why would
anyone want to piss in his backyard,

the physician huffed, explaining
why he would never live in Texas.
I am the moon grinning above the trees.

Have you ever stolen pears for the hell
of it, I asked him.

A LATE LUNCH

A crab cake sandwich, a local amber,
the October wind gusting through the front porch
dining area, the waiter recounting his trek
through the far east when asked—though how
the conversation turned I am not sure—

I sip my ale—here on the Chesapeake edge,
new world colonial houses crowding narrow streets—
I was in Burma, the waiter tells us—he is all of twenty-four—
he smiles with his entire face and asks if we want a refill
on our drinks—I call it Burma in protest, he explains—

Aung San Suu Kyi quietly slips beside us at the table
and then walks us up the street back to our car—
I had forgotten her name, though now I find myself
chanting it—Aung San Suu Kyi—as if a name
could change the course of a stream—

SUNRISE POSE

A poem, she says, is an incantation—
offered up to bring rain or pancakes with maple
syrup. You sleep in late on a Sunday morning
when the roads are quiet and the birds are chirping.
Yesterday, we attended a birthday party.

The girl is walking now—on her toes.
She and her younger cousin bump heads
and looked surprised. They bump
heads again. David talks about the death
of democracy. Clara explains to Charley,

she and Emily have been friends since the first
grade. Ellen tells you she sprained her ankle
when she jumped from the basket of the hot air
balloon after it had touched down, and she is wearing
high heels only now, after several months.

Today will be warmer than yesterday. The wind
is blowing. Somewhere in a church people are praying
for someone to be healed, for absolution, for the world
to be set right, for rain and pancakes with maple syrup.
You sleep in late on a Sunday morning.

INTERSECT

You wait, or you pretend to be waiting,
perhaps in a small room sitting at a table
with a white shiny top, a cup of coffee
and a spoon. The coffee has grown
cold. Just last week you were playing
touch football in the park with a group
of friends, one of those fall days when
the wind picked leaves from the trees,
and John saw you breaking
into the open, that delicious moment
when your eyes connected. But now
you are sitting at a table in a room
waiting quietly for some word.
You listen to the sound of a heater
blowing warm air. You watch
the flight of the ball in the park,
a spot arcing against a grey sky.
You are water simply flowing
to where the arc meets the earth.
A cup of coffee is next to a spoon
on a white table top.
Something has happened,
but you can't remember.

WATER

We load a 2500 gallon rain catcher
on a sixteen foot trailer–lifting
and pushing with aging legs, arms, backs–

lean against the truck bed,
laughing so hard about nearly dying,
trying to catch our breath–gasping
between spasms.

When we were thirty, you kept saying–
But we were never thirty. Six, twelve, seventeen
maybe–

We eat a watermelon cut into quarters.
Squatting on the front porch. We plunge face
first into the fruit. I eat the seeds. You spit them
on the ground.

Our grandfather sits in the front yard
holding a cigarette between his yellowed fingers,
his thumb missing, lost in the teeth of a rip saw
before the Great War–

A rope swing hangs from the limb of a pecan
across the dirt road next to the abandoned car.

Our grandmother, a second wife–the first dying
in the flu epidemic–is on the back porch,
pumping water from a deep well.

SIXTH GRADE WORLD HISTORY

The roads are frozen in spots,
but the schools remain open here.
My wife leaves for work. It will get colder
today. More freezing rain.

Maybe parents with sense, she says
as she starts her car. We both know who
she means. The boy who announces
loudly each day he doesn't have a pencil,

the one who needs more and more
from a well dug deep. She wakes early
to double check lessons, lowers a bucket
into the earth, smiles as she drives away.

WEED

tiny purple blossoms of henbit
ignore the morning freeze,
undesirable in a garden,
but beautiful immigrants nevertheless–

spring in a few weeks
though it's snowing in Tennessee
and New York–here henbit
and dandelion are claiming ground

if it were left to me, I would never
mow my yard–

FAT TUESDAY

We seek comfort in shoelaces and leather–
I run with you in San Diego on a Saturday
morning early from a park somewhere, through
empty streets, the city still sleeping–a gang
of us like antelopes or wolves.

In a coffee shop later a woman smiles and thanks me
for being there as if one could choose not to breathe.
How poignant it seems to me now–the notion
of a single breath, the importance of air–
how we depend so much on what we think ordinary.

My youngest daughter writes instead of giving
something up, she will do yoga for lent as a way
of exploring who and what–If anyone wants to join
me, she says.

AN AWKWARD PAUSE

A spattering of verbs–to laugh at a joke
poorly told, to smile across the room at a woman
you met at a bank reception in November,
she smiles back, and you are committed before
the evening gives way to midnight–

A tug at your sleeve–some guy having
sipped past his quota wants to tell you,
needs really–what an ass you were
the other day–was it a year ago–
when you asked what conclusions

or recommendations could be drawn
from the mountain of data–as if some sense
should be part of the equation–
You were an ass, he says–you nod
and move toward the woman

who is now sipping a white wine and talking
to a man wearing a suede jacket–
The guy unsatisfied blocks your way,
his face flushed red–Who the hell wears suede,
you ask him–an awkward pause–

If we were in Memphis we could probably
just wait for the ducks, you finally say to him.

AN AFTERNOON TEA PARTY

I learned to lie the years I taught in the public schools
from fourteen year old experts who could change a story
in mid sentence without a noticeable increase in heart rate
or breathing. The connection between reality and the spoken
word only incidental, truth telling being an admission of guilt–

and don't believe for a moment that any "coming clean"
is ever the best policy, is ever forgiven.
I am unlocking the door to the weight room with a pass
key I am not authorized to have. Where did you get that key,
the principal says walking up behind me–Shit.

I unlock the door, stash the key in my pocket, then turn
to my principal who is grinning like the Cheshire
in Alice. What key, I ask. Then turn back to the door
and open it. Wow, the door is unlocked, I tell him.
He stares at me, then turns and walks away.

A REFRAIN

Imagine a woman walking in a brown coat
across a parking lot, the wind blowing her hair–
You are a young man, say twenty, and you watch

from a safe distance and chisel the scene in the stone
of your memory. You wait years for her to look
your way, but she is simply walking from class

on a small college campus on the edge of nowhere,
the dust blowing–books cradled in her arm,
her chin tucked into her shoulder for protection.

Nothing happens–no moment when she looks up
and smiles at you–a fulcrum of sorts,
though you can never fully explain.

A YELLOW FOG

I dreamed you alive,
though I don't remember
what you were wearing—
you appear in a crowded
room, glad to see me.

I make my way
toward you, through elbows
and shoulders—
The room tilts, and I lose
you in the confusion.

I wake to the sound of sleet
on the roof, the heater,
my throat dry, the room dark—
no human voices, still
I drown.

AFTER THE PARTY

The only place I want to be anymore,
he writes to Bob who is outside Shanghai,
is on the California beach, under LAX,
watching planes coming in to land,
waiting for the long expected slide
into the Pacific.

Mark writes it's time we storm
the Winter Palace, so to speak,
knowing that even with the qualifier–
somewhere software deciphers
code for Palace, for storm,
for tequila and lime.

There's nothing here but poetry,
Neruda reportedly says, so to speak–
The palace has moved to Dubai,
he says.

EQUILIBRIUM

We can't save the world from the coming storm,
or won't—the same as can't—not even ourselves—
a hardening of arteries—
watching the super bowl and thinking it real.
Cheese served with crackers and a red

from the hill country—telling ourselves we're buying
local. A summer tomato grown in the back yard,
grown under netting to keep birds away,
picked ripe along with a few basil leaves—
A mother tries to nurse her baby—

but her milk has dried. The baby cries without
sound or tears—and God—
is busy building or destroying stars,
a galaxy or two—The woman squats on the ground
holding her child—

GARBAGE DAY

I carry a plastic bag of garbage to the bin
which I roll to the curb, only there is no curb
on our street. I am late, but the truck hasn't come
yet. Good. The ground is wet from days of rain,
wonderful rain. I am barefoot.

When we were children in Puerto Rico,
we were told not to go barefoot–hookworms.
It's only now in late life that I am trying
to feel the ground. I walk across the lawn,
mostly dandelions and other weeds,

cold and wet. I imagine myself connected
to the earth through the souls of my feet.
Inside, on the news, lawmakers are maneuvering
for war, their faces puffed like blowfish.
On-line, someone complains about teachers

being too lazy to teach. I sip my coffee,
my wonderful coffee.

IN THE NIGHT

I have friends–people I know
who look forward to the end with giddy
anticipation, as if things will be made right
for them, though for the life of me–
or for the cabbage of me would make
as much sense–

Those early first century saints
too hungered with anticipation.
Did they die old and disappointed
having miscalculated. I walk down
an empty street in the morning.

I am old with grandchildren who
are learning to walk and talk,
who play on the trampoline
in their back yard. I do not want
their world to end.

Though I know up close that God
can be a first class thief.

LAST REQUEST

He plays the bad seed in the family
narrative. The boy–always thinking,
the old man points and says, his eyes narrowed
into a hardness reserved for what
one truly resents.

The boy balks at taking fish off the hook.
How will you ever raise sons, the man asks
from the back of the boat. I won't,
the boy replies. And after some hesitation,
he grabs the fish.

Chided for attending church as a teen–
for not paying enough heed to honoring
one's father–then for leaving it as a man.
My son doesn't believe in God, his father
complains to neighbors.

He doesn't respect–that much is true.
But when his dying father asks for a cold one,
and his mother offers him a glass of ice
water, he leans in and tells her
a cold one is a beer.

No, his mother says, he's quit drinking.

THE BLESSED

If he had to pick a side,
God knows he hates choosing,
it would be for lovers, especially
the ones not on the formal invitation
list, the unapproved who risk
stones for a flicker of candle light.

Oh, that I were a glove–such divine
idiocy. He could pick cooks though.
Or gardeners. Or the ones who sneak
into the country at night wearing little more
than hope. So much depends
on a breakfast burrito.

He drops a five dollar bill into an open
guitar case. The singer nods.
I once swam naked in a pool at a party
on a dare, his good friend says.
When I realized I was embarrassed,
it was too late.

ROOTS

We are coded the same, you and I–
yet the gulf between us is carved too deep
to span with any bridge. We play half court
basketball in the gym, sweat glistening,
the squeaks of rubber on a wooden floor–

We drink water from the cooler–the same,
you and I–I never loved anyone more.
You set a pick then roll toward the hoop,
the ball floats from me to you, a play
we work as if we were born to it.

You grin and then leave school that spring
because you missed your home too much
to stay. We tried to join a pick up game
that last afternoon in a community gym,
but were told it was a closed set.

Chumps, I muttered, but you walked away.
Nothing ever changes, you said shaking your
head later as we sat on the curb, each
eating a barbeque sandwich sold at a place
only open for lunch.

PRINTS

How, if I am unhappy, do you expect
me to decipher the code—
my being in the room with you
on a Friday morning talking about
the time my father—

What was it. I can't remember
details or the subject anymore,
still you think it important to sort
through old photographs kept
in a box under the stairs.

In one, my brother and I are standing
on the steps of the Capital Building,
December, 1955, pretending we
are lingering–absorbing the sights,
snow falling.

In another, we are buck naked
in a row boat, our mother toweling
us off. We had been swimming
in the cold water, three and four,
photographed in shades of grey.

The boy teaches himself to like tomatoes
on a hamburger with onions and mustard–
His father recuperates in the Army/Navy hospital.
They avoid the wing where the patient
breathing in an iron lung is dying.

His mother leads them up the back stairs.
Is this relevant, I ask. You look up at me,
then at the photograph. My father in full
torso cast. I once kept my brother
from stepping in front of a car, I say.

THURSDAY

A man holds his wife close.
It could have easily been another,
they both know–if circumstance
or whim–Winter gives way to pollen
and rain. She leaves early before school

today. The boys' father is in jail
again, and she needs to run by
with a breakfast taco, or something.
She is an angel, the grandmother says.
He sips his coffee and looks

out the window. A bird chirps
from a power line. The red oak is golden,
an acorn he planted twenty years ago,
its trunk bent from a late night collision
with a truck when it was still a sapling.

He holds his wife close before
she leaves, and tells her–

THINGS FALL APART

An artist, perhaps one of the hapless painters
from after the war when mirrors
were cracked and decency was shown
to be a goon with red eyes and sulfur breath,
painting a world without trees or grass–
He buys a hot dog from the vendor who once

worked the park. He pays with crumpled
bills pulled from his front pocket, the magic
of currency. He paints a world where children
are born old, where nannies speak Russian,
where the trains run on time. He takes the line
away from the city to the coast.

It is cold there. The beaches are empty.
Wrapped in a heavy coat, he sits at his easel
reconstructing a summer lost when he dropped
mustard on his shirt, and she laughed–
not at him, he knows that now. She wore a white
cotton blouse and knew the stars by name.

AIR

The ordinary life begins in the center
and works its way to the edges
in colors of green and brown and red—
You and I walk the track where the high
school team is practicing for the coming

fall. The coach snaps, keep your head
in the game. It's time to turn
back, you tell me. We take the short cut
through the alley—acclimating
to the high air.

We talk about buying bikes and riding
the mountain trails above the town,
but it's enough now to walk laps,
after working the clinic for the day—
people with pains real and imagined.

The ordinary life begins with a breath—
We eat a salad bought at a local Wendy's
and settle in for an episode of Foyle's.

ON A STAR

Only one wish, she says–but whatever
you want. I know the meaning of the word,
he tells her. Maybe to look out from an uncurtained
window down on a London street in October, 1928–
a morning crowd, the hurrying feet–between
the wars, no one reading *Anthony*–

I could wish for that–or for a half court pick up
game on a concrete slab in an Austin park,
November, 1975–or a cheeseburger with mustard
and onions, sharing a six pack of assorted ales
with Bill in July the next year and talking
the sun down, our teeth growing numb.

A policeman shines his light to tell us the park
is closed. But don't ask me to change the world,
he tells her.

LAMPLIGHT

She plays volley ball in the gym
during second period PE wearing maroon
shorts and a white blouse. A grade ahead–
Mangan's sister standing on the steps,
the light from an open door.

He chases a rainbow riding his bike until
a soldier, working under the hood of a truck,
sees him and asks if he's chasing that rainbow.
No, he answers. It's okay, kid, the soldier tells him.
I chased them too. I'm not, he repeats himself.

The rainbow came down only a block away–
So close.

PRUDENCE

He was talked into life insurance policies
on his children when they were young
and premiums were low. To cover expenses,
he was told–believed it wise. Contingency
plans as if one could–

A funeral on the cheap, five thousands
and change–We don't talk
about such things. Never mind creditors
who write and call. It's only their job.
Even after a year or more.

For peace of mind, the commercial says.

KNOWING

He remembers the rage of the strap,
always applied with the assurance he would
understand–someday. He never did.
The ripples of a disturbed mind–
whelps on his back and legs–

It's a wonder you're sane, his aunt
once said of him, when they talked about
why his mother never left. I'm not, he replied.
I'm merely functional–a word he grew
to appreciate by the time he turned fifty.

Three basic rules–don't hit anyone,
stay out of jail, pay your bills.
Is that all it takes, students would ask.
No, he would tell them. It's a beginning.
The rest you learn on the job–

He wanted to tell them more–how she slipped
away at night in her father's stolen car and climbed
through his bedroom window, the rest of the house
asleep, and stayed till almost dawn,
the mingling of sweat and skin–

but those are secrets you must discover on your own
if you are to know them.

HOW COULD WE NOT

Mom said I could go, she says ready to leave,
but let's go out the back door—
this girl who takes on her older sister's name
when she is four, who watches dance recital
videos for hours when she is three
and dances to them—

You can call me Lou, she tells her dance instructor
who looks quizzically at my wife—
She is a dog for a while, until she tastes
the food, then decides she is a girl again.
I watch her walking up a sidewalk from school,
carrying her backpack at six—

the image of her carrying that heavy bag chiseled
in my brain. In a Boston trip, on a bus,
she asks me what language the driver is speaking—
English, I tell her. She listens more attentively—
She visits the Louvre and tells me it is too much
to absorb in a single day—She sits beside me

in a car while driving the Interstate in a hard
rain. Her mother comes out the front door
to say goodbye—She didn't say I could go,
she didn't say I could go, she says having been caught—
But we let her go anyway, didn't we, my wife says.
How could we not—

REDEMPTION 1

Why do you think you can make things right?
she asked me in a tone with sharp edges.
I am a wizard, I might have said,
or an angel, as I once told my grandmother
who didn't remember anymore who I was,
but who had wondered about the wings
as we sat outside on a bench
near the boxwood hedges, and she winked
at me… my grandmother.

And who are you honey? she asked me again
after the moment with the angel had passed.
I am an angel, I told her again in a whisper.
That's right…she said more with her eyes
than her voice, pale eyes that saw
past the surface of things.
I was wondering about the wings, wasn't I.

And can you see them? I asked her,
the one I was with, not my grandmother,
or might have asked her had I told her
who I was, who I really was
and why I had to make things right,
but she wasn't interested in angels,
and she couldn't see the wings.

REDEMPTION 2

The day begins with melting snow
and a cello playing the story line
in a tango by Piazzolla.
You and I have danced it a hundred times.

The cello though is against the wall,
a rule ignored, if only for a moment,
as you are adjusting to the cold air,
and we both hear the crack.

I see it in your eyes, the cello
on the floor broken in a hundred
pieces or more, but really only a line
running with the grain on the back.

Still, it will have to be repaired,
the man who knew cellos says
in a voice that dances in harmony
with the Bach concerto playing in the next room.

And he gives you a new cello
for the interim. A new cello without a crack.
And even though we forget it and have to go back,
the day seems right for us.

At least while there is snow on the ground.

REDEMPTION 3

Do you believe in redemption,
my daughter asks. She sips her hot
chocolate and looks at me.
Your mother doesn't forgive me
if that's what you mean, I answer.

The morning snow has melted,
and we are sitting at a table in the sun,
warming our hands with hot chocolate and coffee,
pretending the sun is enough
to warm the rest of us.

I watched a man adjust the bridge of a cello
this morning, I tell my daughter,
and I watched a woman admire this man
who knew things and had grown comfortable
with the place he had made for himself.

When I noticed a crack in the instrument,
he simply said it would need to be repaired,
as if that settled the matter.
No redemption is necessary, I tell her.
She understands.

I think maybe it's simply getting good at something.
or knowing something well. Or loving it.
She smiles at me as if to tell me
words could work at times,
if one is sitting in the sun after the snow has melted.

LESSONS OF THE OWL: PART THREE

She dips into her purse
as if it were her heart
and retrieves a five dollar bill
she exchanges for a red sucker
the man on the corner is hawking
or was it the purple one.

I am going to save the world
from child abuse she once told him,
but she really finds more comfort
walking in the sand on the Texas coast
watching the waves of the gulf
and listening for the voices of mermaids.

So he dips into his heart
as if it were a purse
and whispers in her ear
between the splashing of the waves.
This is saving the world, he tells her

PASSING

When they are all dead,
there will be no one
left to stand witness,
not that testimonies
are ever believed if inconvenient.
And even when acknowledged,
the grey realities
of boxcars crammed
with shopkeepers and poets,
children and lunatics,
are easily dismissed
when an American president
lays a wreath at a cemetery
honoring the goons
of the twentieth century.
And when the last
of them disappear from
the earth, the ones who saw
the skeletons, breathing and still,
the ones who were there
and know, when they are gone,
how long will it be before
we are told to reconsider.

SLOW DANCING

Sometimes, when you're lucky,
you get the timing down just right.
The band plays in the gym.
She sits in the bleachers
with her seventh grade students.

He stands on the sidelines,
next to the speech teacher.
The band plays its final number,
a slow tune, and people dance.

She expects him to dance with someone
else. He calmly walks over to where
she is sitting and holds out his hand.

Laura calls it race horse timing
in her poem. Whatever, it was good,
and she danced with him
in front of the entire school.

THE LEDGER

Sonny was murdered yesterday.
They found him in his car
wrecked on the side of the road,
an ATM receipt on the seat beside him,
a bullet hole in his chest,
and blood everywhere.
They figured he was trying
to drive himself to a hospital
or somewhere to get help,
but he died instead.
And we talked about how Sonny
had grown chickens in the backyard
of the house he rented from us
a couple of years ago.
Home grown chickens
just taste different, he would explain.
And he paid his rent most of the time.
Except toward the end,
when his wife left him.

STOPPING FOR LUNCH AT A STRIP MALL DELI

I generally have a way with older men,
she said as she ordered her sandwich,
an item not on the menu,
creating consultations and considerations
among the staff when finally
the cook gazed across the counter
and declared if she could describe it
he sure as hell could make it.

He knew she was only taking coup,
a way of declaring space for herself,
and after eating only a bite
she was ready to leave.

TURKISH COFFEE GROUNDS

A shaman approaches him at a basketball game
offering to decipher his character
by reading the discarded peanuts shells
around his feet.

Tea leaves and coffee grounds
can serve as well,
the shaman says, but here we only have
the shells of peanuts.

And the price, he asks.
What is the price of a soul,
the spirit dancer replies.

I ONCE BUILT HOUSES

It could have been art–the handling of wood
on a morning after a light rain when the puddles
lay on the slab revealing secrets not seen
on a hot dry day,
walking the top plates
like tight rope dancers,
balancing on the slick wet surfaces
of two by fours, daring the fates,
if there were such things,
Daedalus and Icarus,
he and another squatting on opposite sides
of an open air room, lining up words like joists and rafters.
It's all in the speaking of it, he says.

It could have been art–but when the woman calls
on a morning after she had moved in and lived for a year
or more in the comfort of sunshine filtering through curtains,
art gives way to more important matters.
I want you to see, she says, taking them into the room
where under a vanity cabinet, in a shadow tucked away
where it could be seen only
when one sitting on the porcelain throne
cracks the chamber door,
a nail hole, a small divot.

There, she says pointing to the flaw in the syntax,
one easily seen by a careful reader.
I was happy until then, she tells them,
her voice melting wax.

THE DEATH OF KONG

The old man walks out of the market
with a boxed salad in hand, brushes against
a large smooth stone bordering a gravel
filled stream, constructed to run between
the tables of the patio, and stumbles.

I didn't think the man was going to fall.
He merely brushes against the rock,
but his balance has left him,
and like Kong he teeters for a second
and then falls face first into the gravel
and shallow water, holding the boxed salad,
a kind of impersonation of Faye Wray,
though Kong had the good sense
to put her down before the plunge.

People rush to the old man's aid.
First people from the tables nearby
and then the ones from the market.
Ice and bandages are offered,
a fresh salad box.

The man sits on the edge of the stream,
embarrassed. His wife pretends
she isn't with him.

PLAYING THE RULES

Speak in tongues, the king's if you wish
an audience, but don't think for a second–not one
blip–a letter of recommendation written
by an old professor who understood the difference
between the good and the ugly. He takes a sip.

If only he had not talked about his wife so freely,
or his children–Thank God, he was silent concerning
the woman on the elevator whose hand brushed
his ever so slightly. He was clever enough,
had read the cannons, written extensively

about the failure of words–the citizens of Melos,
a farewell address–only sounds. But he simply
didn't measure up, his father's hands too rough
from picking cotton in the bottoms next to the river–
before the war.

Leo calls for the ball and cuts it with the edge
of his belt buckle, no one the wiser.

DRY BREAD AND COFFEE

He poses as an old friend
driving in the neighborhood by chance.
She opens the door, puts on a face
that pretends she's glad to see him—

offers a cup of coffee and a slice of bread,
baked yesterday, a little dry—
but it's all I have, she says. He nods.
She measures the coffee grounds
with a spoon. She once took a certain
delight in the taste of coffee on his breath—

but that was before either of them had read
Virginia, before either had learned the difference
between a fiction clinging by a spider's
thread and the narrative they actually live.

The coffee is brewing,
she slices the bread with a knife,
then, standing at the counter,
showing herself in profile, she sighs almost.
This is my life, she says gesturing
to the dishes piled in the sink.

Somewhere in the threads of a spider's web,
somewhere between the coffee and bread,
sitting at a table and passing time,
comparing the sun weathered spots on their arms,
dancing to the sounds of an old friendship
that had once meant more, had once meant dangling
from a second story window and dropping
into the bushes below, somewhere in the exchange,
she tries to explain, as if one could make sense of it.

As much as I was ever capable of love, she tells him.

SUNDAY

It is hard to believe we will die,
despite the weight of evidence,
that all this will cease to matter—

poems and rain, slicing a watermelon
in June and eating the juicy
meat, seeds and all.

All of this—angels are in the room,
I tell you, holding your arm,
my face pressed close to yours.

PARTING

John and Leopold share Henrys in a way,
both naughty, though one is quite willing
to jump your bones if only your husband
weren't present in the room, while the other
is content with a letter, knowing he will
never see you, never touch–

There are laws against both–of decency,
written on parchment with a feathered pen.
How to begin–you and I as we make our way
down corridors crowded with paintings,
Degas and his dancers. Manet–we are both
in love with Morisot.

Beauty flickers–the battery runs down,
and you look for an outlet somewhere.
I try to explain that one summer we laid
Mexican brick in straight lines, trowelling
the mortar liberally and tapping into place
each piece, the sun unmercifully hot.

You dip your finger in cold water
and touch it to my lips. We drink beer
at a café on 24th street between the wars,
before the weddings, before the children
were born, before decorating the Christmas
tree–

You try to explain the afternoon you met
me in the park to tell me–we are both
in love with Morisot, but it isn't enough.

HOLDING STILL

Unspoken words
to be delivered
on a Friday afternoon.
We listen–We wait,
the urgency gone out
of it for now. Gunned down,
riding the back
seat–hands flutter.
I imagine sitting
at a window above
the street, on a knoll,
at the curb–anywhere.
In a balcony eating
popcorn.

A disconnect when
what was never supposed
to happen–We keep watch,
kiss in the front seat
at a drive-in,
as if kissing would glue
the pieces back in place,
your face glowing
in moonlight, your face
now lost to me.
We keep watch–an act
of faith, we say.
Standing the night,
waiting for dawn.

You write me from Spain,
from Egypt, from Tokyo–
Once ran the bulls
in Pamplona, but it wasn't
the same. I meant
to write back,
but mowed the lawn instead
and cooked hamburgers
on the grill. We stood watch
one night and held the earth
in orbit, one Friday
after they cancelled
play practice when words
bled down the page.

FRIDAY

He counts the buds on a dying
oak, seeking signs that it may live
at least another year–at least.

Suddenly here, mowed grass
and Spring. Marries in April.
April, his father dies, a daughter born.

It's time, she whispers in his ear
after services, and he feels–
the beginning and end of rain

and bluebonnets and coffee beans.
She whispers it's time–
Do you love me, he asks

in the morning after the children
have grown, in the morning before
toast and jam. Of course, she says.

ONLY THE RAIN

Who else could play your part so well,
you ask, as if the matter could be settled
with a word, as if the patterns of our lives
were merely raindrops on leaves.

It's only the rain, you say,
only the rain falling,
only the rain.

Notes, references, and allusions–

The poet dances shirtless in the heat of the day. He dances with the sun, with the rain, with henbits blooming in early spring, with every person he has known, every painting he has seen, every song he has heard, every book he has read.

Dust –The opening line echoes T. S. Eliot's open lines in "The Burial of the Dead" with the words *April, breeding*, and *out of the*. The rhythm is similar, I think. In the forth stanza: *So much depends* refers to William Carlos Williams's "The Red Wheelbarrow." This phrase is repeated in several poems.

The Light in an Aging House–Degas gets the credit for the woman with the russet sponge being in *Le Tub*. Susanna Childress also has a very good poem about the woman with the russet sponge in "The Hyssop Tub."

The Fall–The Madame Pericand and Jacqueline scene comes from *Suite Française* by Irène Némirovsky. The narrator in the poem is reading the book in a coffee shop.

When All Else Fails–*all the king's horses, all the king's men* refers to the nursery rhyme Humpty Dumpty.

MoMA–While the title refers to the Museum of Modern Art in New York City, the poem does not reference any particular painting.

Om–Again here are allusions to "The Red Wheelbarrow."

Moloch–Moloch appears in Alan Ginsberg's *Howl*. Kurt Vonnegut survived the bombing of Dresden and wrote about it in *Slaughterhouse Five*.

literary criticism during and after the war–The central character in this poem is loosely based on Walter Benjamin, though he morphs momentarily into a Rainer Maria Rilke character in a line or two. There is also a echo of Borges's map.

Asylum–This poem references Anne Sexton's "Walking in Paris" and an untitled poem dated November 9,1970. The narrator is reading through her poems scattered on the floor.

Writing Its Own History–References Che Guevara's execution. The title come from Guevara's 1964 speech at the United Nations.

if ever–References the Rick Roderick lectures on philosophy.

Sand Creek–References the massacre at Sand Creek on November 29, 1864.

Pinned–Miranda and Frederick are characters in John Fowles's *The Collector*. Jim Knox is a Texas Ranger announcer.

Necessity–References Annie Dillard's "Living Like Weasels."

In Dreams–References John Berryman's *Dream Songs* and the death of Delmore Schwartz. It also makes a reference to Schwartz's "In Dreams Begin Responsibilities."

skimmers–References Elizabeth Kolbert's *The Sixth Extinction.*

A Confession–References *St. Augustine's Confessions.*

A Late Lunch–*Aund San Suu Kyi* is a key opposition figure in Myanmar.

A Yellow Fog–References T. S. Eliot's "The Love Song of Alfred J. Prufrock." Both the title and the last two lines of the poem but with a twist.

The Blessed–Echoes from Romeo *Oh, that I were a glove.* Again *so much depends* alludes to "The Red Wheelbarrow."

Air–A Reference to the BBC series "Foyle's War."

On a Star–The scene in London references the scene in Virginia Woolf's *A Room of One's Own.*

Lamplight–Mangan's sister is a character in James Joyce's "Araby."

Passing–The president lays a wreath echoes sentiments in Steve Erickson's *The Sea Came in at Midnight.*

Slow Dancing–References Laura Telford's poem "How The Almost Famous Preacher Handled the Small Funeral for the Son of a Past Friend."

Dry Bread and Coffee–The spider's thread comes from Virginia Woolf's *In a Room of One's Own.*

Parting–Alludes to John Berryman's *Dream Songs* and Leopold Bloom's alter ego in James Joyce's *Ulysses.* Berthe Morisot was a painter and a model who appears in the paintings of Manet.

About the Author

Brady Peterson lives near Belton, Texas where for much of the past thirty years he worked building houses or teaching rhetoric and literature at a local university. He once worked a fork lift in a lumber yard in East Austin, tried to teach eighth graders the importance of using language, worked briefly as a technical writer, and helped raise five daughters. He has run one marathon, fought in one karate tournament, climbed one mountain, failed to make the UT baseball team as a walk on, and took tango lessons with his wife. He is the author of *Glued to the Earth* and *Between Stations*.